ESSEN...

C000170840

Exp...

MULTIMEDIA

ESSENTIAL TIPS

Exploring

MULTIMEDIA

TECHNICAL CONSULTANT
Chris Lewis

DORLING KINDERSLEY
London • New York • Sydney • Moscow

A DORLING KINDERSLEY BOOK

Editor Fiona Wild
Art Editor Alan McKee
Senior Editor Gillian Roberts
Series Art Editor Alison Donovan
Picture Researcher Sam Ruston
Production Controller Hélène Lamassoure

The full names of certain products referred to in this book are:
Microsoft® MS-DOS®, Microsoft® Windows® 95, MSN™, The Microsoft® Network,
Microsoft® Internet Gaming Zone, Microsoft® Internet Explorer, Microsoft® Encarta 97.
Netscape Communications, the Netscape Communications logo, Netscape &
Netscape Navigator are trademarks of Netscape Communications Corporation.

Every effort has been made to trace the copyright holders.
The publisher apologizes for any unintentional omissions and would be pleased,
in such cases, to place an acknowledgment in future editions of this book.

First published in Great Britain in 1997 by
Dorling Kindersley Limited,
9 Henrietta Street, London WC2E 8PS

Visit us on the World Wide Web at http://www.dk.com

A CIP catalogue record for this book is available from the British Library

ISBN 0-7513-0480-8

Text film output by The Right Type, Great Britain
Reproduced by Colourscan, Singapore
Printed and bound by Graphicom, Italy

ESSENTIAL TIPS

WHAT IS MULTIMEDIA?

1 MULTIMEDIA EXPLAINED

Multimedia combines many types of media into a single package – text, pictures, animation, video, and sound. It is also interactive, involving the user in selection and control. Multimedia computers can produce hi-fi sound, 3-D graphics, photo-realistic pictures, film footage, and animation. They are powerful educational tools, offer crucial business services, and provide the ultimate in home entertainment.

△ STORYBOOKS (TIP 46)

▷ LANGUAGE LEARNING (TIP 44)

VIDEOCONFERENCING (TIP 100) ▷

△ CARTOONS (TIP 42)

△ 3-D ACTION: MARATHON II (BUNGIE)

2 WHAT DOES INTERACTIVE MEAN?

Multimedia gives you the chance to influence what appears on the screen. Interactive features range from simple selection from a list of options, to question and answer, to directing a film plot. *Virtual Reality Cat* (Dorling Kindersley) offers numerous interactive options.

VIRTUAL REALITY CAT
In this realistic 3-D museum, objects can be selected and even rotated, like this cheetah's skull.

3 WHO USES MULTIMEDIA?

Everyone has something to gain from multimedia. At home, multimedia, such as CD-Roms, provide a source of entertainment and education, from reference works (for example, encyclopedias) to action-packed games. In business, companies may use multimedia for training, for presentations, and in general communications.

Today's electronic schemes enable trainees to work unsupervised and at their own pace, choosing their subject areas

Trainees monitor their own progress by recording modules studied. The title also evaluates skill and performance.

TRAINING SCHEMES
Leading Teams, *from Xebec, is an interactive, module-based program for trainee managers.*

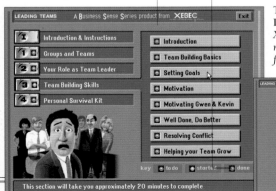

4 COMMERCIAL APPLICATIONS

In business and public service, multimedia has an important role to play. The task of presenting information to clients, staff, and the general public is increasingly being handed over to interactive multimedia, which can teach, inform, promote, and sell in new ways that are both more effective for the organization and more entertaining for the user. Interactive kiosks can now be found in more and more locations including shops, offices, museums, and even aeroplanes. Some of the kiosk services offered by the Smithsonian Institution in Washington, DC, are shown in this example.

▷ **INTERACTIVE TOUR GUIDE**
Kiosks help visitors find their way around, and offer information on exhibitions and facilities. The system works in several languages.

▽ **SCREEN TEST**
Starting at the main menu, visitors use a touch screen to find out information about the Smithsonian, from videos of new exhibits to the location of cafés.

Touch Here For English

Para Español Presione Aquí

日本語はここに手を入れてください。

Pour Le Français, Appuyer Ici

Für Deutsch Bitte Hier Drücken

要看中文請按此處

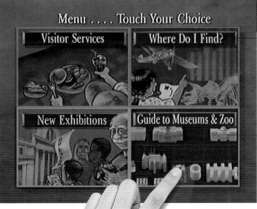

Menu .... Touch Your Choice

Visitor Services

Where Do I Find?

New Exhibitions

Guide to Museums & Zoo

Touching this button allows visitors to track down specific exhibits.

Pressing one of the buildings on the map reveals more options on displays and services.

5 ANALOGUE & DIGITAL

Most current media machines – television sets, video recorders, radios, telephones – are analogue, transmitting information by electrical voltage. Digital machines such as computers and many cellular telephones transmit information in the form of electronic code, and are the key to the multimedia revolution. Words, sound, pictures, video, and numbers are all converted into an electronically intelligible code.

PAINTING BY NUMBERS

6 COMPACT DISCS

The audio compact disc stores a stream of electronic code that represents sound waves. During manufacture, digital data is stamped onto an aluminium disc in the form of hollows (pits) and flat areas (lands), representing the two digits (1 and 0) of binary code. To play a CD, a laser beam is passed over the spinning disc and reflected light patterns are then translated back into data. Discs do not deteriorate with playing as only light touches the disc surface, and the user may jump from track to track at will. CDs prepared the way for CD-Roms, which hold pictures and text in digitized form.

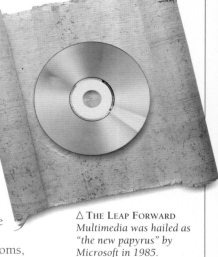

△ THE LEAP FORWARD
Multimedia was hailed as "the new papyrus" by Microsoft in 1985.

MULTI-VOLUME ENCYCLOPEDIA

7 CD-ROM

Compact discs with read-only memory (Rom) were a logical development from the music CD. Their storage capacity is incredible: a single CD-Rom can hold more than two complete sets of the *Encyclopedia Britannica*.

8 CHOOSING EQUIPMENT

Until the information super-highway brings multimedia into every home through a socket, you will need to find space for video recorders, games consoles, CD players, and multimedia computers in your home. Before you buy, it's a good idea to sort out answers to some key questions.

- Will you be using the computer mainly for games?
- Will you need sound or video cards to run fast games titles?
- Do you need a home office for business, or for leisure activities?
- What is the minimum memory you need to have?
- Can you upgrade the system?
- Will you want a modem and Internet connection?
- Would an interactive TV and set-top box best suit your needs?

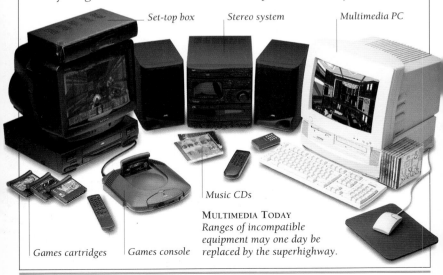

Set-top box

Stereo system

Multimedia PC

Music CDs

MULTIMEDIA TODAY
Ranges of incompatible equipment may one day be replaced by the superhighway.

Games cartridges

Games console

9 APPLE MACINTOSH OR PC?

IBM launched its first desktop computer in 1981 and adopted the term "personal computer", or PC, as the machine's brand name. With the introduction of IBM lookalikes, PC has come to mean any machine that runs the same programs as an IBM PC. The Apple Macintosh, launched in 1984, brought about a completely new use for computers: desktop publishing. Apple Macs are now used in publishing, in schools, and in making multimedia, but in business the PC still rules.

10 MULTIMEDIA PC

The PC became a multimedia machine in the late 1980s, with a processor (the 386) fast enough to handle moving graphics, and a sound card to play back music and speech. Until this point both the sound card and a CD-Rom drive had been optional extras. When the price of CD-Rom drives also became affordable, the multimedia PC had arrived.

Multimedia machines are constantly being updated to make them faster and more powerful, and these days most PCs come with multimedia hardware such as CD-Rom drives already built in. Every few years, a new generation of microprocessor chips comes along that doubles computer power.

▽ THE PC
Nowadays the PC is the world's most popular multimedia machine.

Early machines were monochrome, although a graphics card could add some shades. PCs can now display millions of colours.

Most PCs sold today include a CD-Rom drive

Where once the PC held only a single speaker, all multimedia-ready PCs have stereo sound capability.

The mouse, which transfers commands to the screen, is now an essential feature.

Keyboard

11 MICROSOFT® WINDOWS® 95

The operating system is the computer's master control software, managing the disk drives, keyboard, and screen, and running programs. The operating system Microsoft Windows 95 made PCs very user-friendly, preparing for the development of multimedia software with support such as sound cards and CD-Rom drives. Today, Windows operates on over 80 per cent of the world's PCs.

PC OPERATING SYSTEM

12 UPGRADING SYSTEMS

By the late 1980s, multimedia support elements such as sound cards and CD-Rom drives had become affordable, and were sold together, with speakers, as an "upgrade kit". Now, most PCs come with multimedia hardware already built in, and you are more likely to need upgrades and add-ons such as Internet connections, modems, graphics accelerators, and additional memory (RAM).

▽ GRAPHICS CARD
Graphics technology has leapt ahead: anyone can now use software designed for engineers and architects.

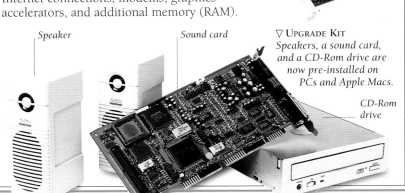

Speaker   Sound card   ▽ UPGRADE KIT
Speakers, a sound card, and a CD-Rom drive are now pre-installed on PCs and Apple Macs.

CD-Rom drive

13 SOFTWARE

Software divides into two main categories – operating systems and programs. Programs range from productive tools such as word processors (known as applications), to multimedia titles for information or entertainment. Programs are stored on the hard disk, floppy disk, or on CD-Rom.

CD-ROM SOFTWARE

14 MONITORS

The monitor turns patterns of voltages from the graphics card into patterns of light. The display area of a monitor is made up of a grid of picture elements (pixels, for short): each is three tiny phosphor dots. The sharpness of the picture depends on the monitor and graphics card.

Three guns fire electron beams at the screen. The strength of each beam is controlled by the signal from the graphics card.

This sheet of metal has tiny holes, designed so that as one beam goes through, it hits only red pixel dots at the front; the second hits green, the third, blue.

An average monitor "colours in" a grid of up to 750,000 pixels to draw each image on the screen.

A pixel is a group of three coloured dots of phosphor that glow when the electron beams hit them. Different colours are made by varying beam strength.

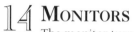
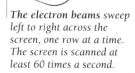

The electron beams sweep left to right across the screen, one row at a time. The screen is scanned at least 60 times a second.

15 MULTIMEDIA IMAGES

Compared with hard disks, CD-Rom drives are frustratingly slow at transferring data from disk to processor. This is particularly noticeable with video, which may look jerky, or can be displayed only in a tiny window. Developers have come up with various ways of disguising the fact that most video clips play in small windows rather than taking up the full screen. One solution is to blend the clip into a larger image that acts as a border. Some titles have optional "enlarge" buttons that will play larger video clips on a more powerful system.

▷ **VIDEO PERFORMANCE**
Digital video rarely takes up the whole screen, but the size of the window showing the video clip is increasing as technology advances.

VIDEO COMPRESSION
Video clips can now be downloaded from many Web sites (Tip 79). To view them, you'll need to download and install the appropriate plug-in software, for example Apple QuickTime (Tip 88, audio & video).

16 ON-LINE FEATURES

Newer generations of CD-Roms now incorporate an on-line link that connects you to a Web site (*Tip 79*) on the Internet. To use the Web site address, connect to the Internet. You need to have a Web browser (*Tip 81*) installed to do this. Run the browser software, which will paste the Web site address into your browser's Internet address field. Electronic magazines can be accessed in this way.

17 FINDING YOUR WAY

Multimedia reference titles can be used to access information in ways that would be impossible with printed books. Not only can designers incorporate animations, videos, sound, and speech along with written information; they can also provide hypertext and hotspot links that allow the user to search for specific information or explore a topic more generally. Just as you can flip from track to track on a music CD, so you can jump from one topic to another on CD-Rom.

WORLDS TO EXPLORE
This example from Dorling Kindersley's Eyewitness Encyclopedia of Nature 2 shows how to navigate.

The naturalist's console is the control centre and starting point of the program. To explore, click on any image shown here.

Clicking on the Mammals poster brings it to the centre screen. Clicking on Catlike Carnivores takes you to more detail.

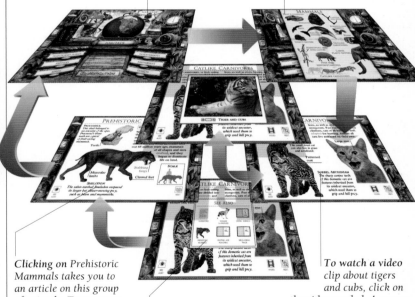

Clicking on Prehistoric Mammals takes you to an article on this group of animals. To return to the main screen, click outside the open window. Some newer CD-Roms also have on-line links.

The See Also box displays a list of related topics to explore.

To watch a video clip about tigers and cubs, click on the video symbol. A screen pops up with a video controller that you click on to play the clip.

WHAT IS A FISH?
A wall poster behind the "desk" displays a menu of topics relating to fish. Each fish points to a different entry in the encyclopedia.

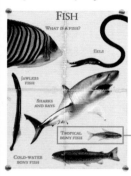

FISH

WHAT IS A FISH?

EELS

JAWLESS FISH

SHARKS AND RAYS

TROPICAL BONY FISH

COLD-WATER BONY FISH

▷ *Clicking on Tropical Bony Fish takes you to the subject entry page, which holds written and spoken information, video, and more cross-referencing.*

▷ *See Also takes you to related topics such as the nature of fish, their habitat, and how they coexist with other forms of life.*

▽ *Selecting a fish or plant brings you to another screen with more information on that species.*

18 RETRIEVING INFORMATION

In most multimedia titles a small pointer on the screen – usually the shape of a hand or arrow – follows the movements of the mouse. Choices are presented on-screen as words or pictures, and choosing between them is simple, you just point with the mouse and click the mouse button. Information is built into a graphical world known as an interface. The main screen of Dorling Kindersley's *Eyewitness Encyclopedia of Nature* is a naturalist's desk, complete with globe, posters, barometer, and reference books.

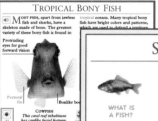

TROPICAL BONY FISH

▽ EXPLORING TOPICS

MOST FISH, apart from jawless fish and sharks, have a skeleton made of bone. The greatest variety of these bony fish is found in tropical oceans. Many tropical bony fish have bright colors and patterns, which are used to defend a territory.

Protruding eyes for good forward vision

Pectoral fin

Boxlike body

COWFISH
This coral reef inhabitant has coxlike facial features.

SEE ALSO

WHAT IS A FISH?

COLD-WATER BONY FISH

EELS

CORAL REEF

COASTS AND CORAL REEFS

SYMBIOSIS

◁ *In this underwater habitat, a coral reef is the graphical home to a number of plant and animal species. You can move about the reef, home in on details, and click on the creatures to find out more about them.*

Clown Triggerfish

THE CONTRASTING patterns of the clown triggerfish are probably used to confuse prey and to warn off any predators. If threatened, the fish retreats and wedges itself under a rock. It does this by locking its dorsal spine – the "trigger" of its name – into an upright position, so that it cannot be dragged from its hiding place.

Dorsal "trigger" spine

Dramatic patterns

BONY FACTS

GO TO TROPICAL BONY FISH

GREAT BARRIER REEF

19 FINDING HOTSPOTS

A hotspot is an on-screen button or picture that reacts when you select it – by taking you to another related part of the title, for instance. Hotspots can be invisible, only revealed by exploring the screen and noticing where the pointer (usually an arrow) changes shape. Hot text is a word or phrase appearing in a different colour.

▽ VOYAGER'S MAKING MAUS
This title makes full use of hotspots. Choices are presented as words or pictures, and selection is by clicking.

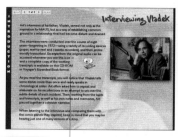

INTERVIEWING VLADEK

Selection of the hotspot Interviewing Vladek takes you to a screen with video clips and an interview transcript. Other hotspots are shown below.

Introduction

Background research

Page layout

Pencil artwork

Multimedia conversion

20 WHAT IS HYPERTEXT?

The most important aspect of multimedia is interactivity – not merely accessing information, but being able to navigate through it, play with it, and sometimes even create something new. Text-based software titles provide the widest opportunity to make use of hypertext, by adding features enabling you to work on the text, make notes in the margin, mark pages and cross-references, and copy passages, all without defacing the original text for another reader.

21 WORKING WITH HYPERTEXT

Text-based titles on CD-Rom are designed to do much more than printed text. Follow up references that interest you by clicking on highlighted words or by using a search menu. Some text titles allow you to attach electronic "paperclips" as temporary bookmarks, with Progress Markers to show how much has been read.

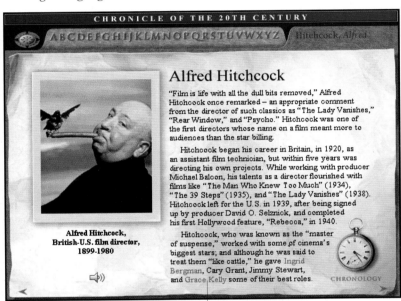

CHRONICLE OF THE 20TH CENTURY
This Dorling Kindersley title covers both World Wars, people, film, and news.

Words or names picked out in red are hotspots (Tip 19), and take you to other related parts of the title.

22 HEALTH & SAFETY

The competitive nature of many computer games means that they can have an addictive, compulsive effect. Ensure that you do not sit in front of the computer screen for extended periods without taking regular breaks.

TAKE SCREEN BREAKS

REFERENCE

23 THE HOME LIBRARY

Most current multimedia titles are designed for home use. Traditional reference books such as encyclopedias and atlases adapt well to multimedia, and reference is the oldest and still the most popular use for CD-Rom-based multimedia. In fact, figures for sales of multimedia encyclopedias now exceed those for printed versions. CD-Roms on leisure topics can offer much more flexibility than books, with the capacity of video and animation to demonstrate practical skills like carpentry or landscape design, or sports such as football and golf.

△ MINE OF INFORMATION
Animations, videos, sound, and speech all add to the presentation of words.

▽ ENCARTA 97 (MICROSOFT®)

VOYAGES OF DISCOVERY
Multimedia reference titles are constantly being refined and developed to allow easier access to stores of knowledge.

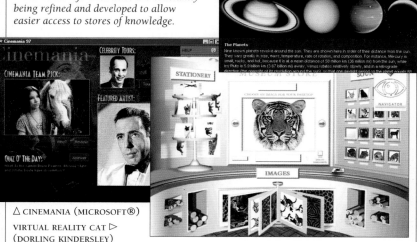

△ CINEMANIA (MICROSOFT®)

VIRTUAL REALITY CAT ▷
(DORLING KINDERSLEY)

24 ONE-SUBJECT ENCYCLOPEDIAS

General encyclopedias have long been a standard for CD-Rom, but an increasing number of titles focus on just one subject. Being narrower in scope, single-subject encyclopedias can go into far more detail. Dorling Kindersley's *Eyewitness Encyclopedia of Nature 2*, shown here, uses a naturalist's console as its main starting screen, which acts as a kind of visual contents list. Just click to explore.

◁ *The fossil* links you to a section on prehistoric life, with features on the earliest-known plants and animals.

△ *Look at* the living world in miniature by selecting the microscope. The Green Book underneath looks at environmental issues.

△ *Choosing the word* Classification brings you to an animated guide that explains how living kingdoms are grouped.

△ EYEWITNESS ENCYCLOPEDIA OF NATURE 2

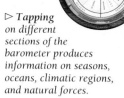

◁ **Rotate the globe** to zoom in and look at ten natural habitats, such as grassland, coral reef, or tundra; or choose from the pull-down list.

◁ **Posters** behind the console represent menus for two classes of animal – fish and mammals. The Fish poster points you towards five main types of fish.

▷ **Tapping** on different sections of the barometer produces information on seasons, oceans, climatic regions, and natural forces.

△ **Look at life** through the eyes of different species with the Animal Vision activity. Here, observe what a Mantis shrimp sees, viewing its prey.

△ **The multi-faceted index** lists every topic, video, animation, and animal sound covered in the Encyclopedia of Nature 2.

25 INTERACTIVE BOOKS

Many interactive book titles take popular novels and add simple interactivity to the text. Voyager's *Expanded Books* series adds hypertext (*Tip 20*), though no animation or sound, to enable readers to make notes in the margin, look up key words and phrases, and mark text.

A NEW GENERATION OF BOOKS

▽ 3-D ATLAS (MULTIMEDIA CORPORATION)
The main screen features a globe which can be rotated to access information.

26 ATLASES

Multimedia atlases present the same information as a printed atlas but in a more dynamic and involving way. Countries are brought to "real" life with sound, animations, satellite and time-lapse photography, and video clips. Titles usually include maps, illustrations, tables, and statistical data. You can view whole countries or individual regions, and specific information about places can be manipulated and displayed in a number of different ways.

▽ NAVIGATE THE GLOBE
You can point to any area and zoom in via the plus button. The globe displayed may be environmental, physical, or political.

27 USING A 3-D ATLAS

The *3-D Atlas* (Multimedia Corporation) contains numerous related video clips and animation. The clips include documentary videos about major environmental issues such as acid rain and over-fishing, and fly-throughs of habitats, for example rainforest and tundra.

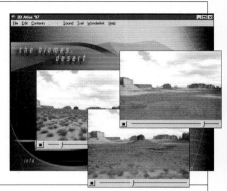

ANIMATED FLY-THROUGH

28 ZOOMING IN ON FEATURES

With *3-D Atlas*, you can zoom in on satellite images of some of the world's major cities, including New York, San Francisco, London, Moscow, and Tokyo. This example takes the viewer closer and closer to the river Thames in London.

CLOSE-UP VIEWS

29 STATISTICS MADE EASY

Statistical information can be presented in various ways in *3-D Atlas*. Shown here are examples of a scatter chart and a ranking table. You could also compile statistical line charts and globe charts.

SCATTER CHART

RANKING TABLE

30 INTERACTIVE MUSEUMS

Visiting a modern museum or art gallery is perhaps the original multimedia experience – a blend of images, sound, animations, and video. Dorling Kindersley's *Eyewitness Virtual Reality Dinosaur Hunter* presents an artificial museum complete with museum-like displays. A Dinosaur Excavation Site enables you to go digging for dinosaur fossils and even to assemble skeletons, bringing dinosaurs "back to life".

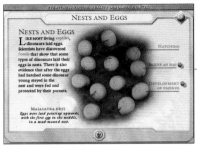

△ *Clicking on different parts of the screen will take you to further related screens, with animations such as the hatching of a dinosaur egg. The footprint at the base of the screen links to topics like Nesting.*

VIRTUAL MUSEUM
This title includes quizzes, a "shop", maps of dinosaur fossil find sites, and a Web site link.

△ *Clicking on Navigator takes you to a museum map, from which you can jump instantly to any part of the complex.*

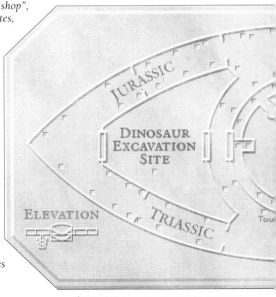

△ VIRTUAL REALITY DINOSAUR HUNTER

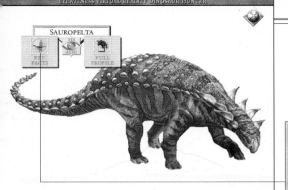

▽ *Selecting Key Facts will bring you to a screen with a summary of the essential information about a species. Full Profile takes you to a much more detailed account.*

SAUROPELTA
KEY FACTS

Sauropelta was a four-legged plant-eater that was protected by armour made up from bony plates, cones, and studs.

TIME:	*114–97 MYA*
SIZE:	*Length 7.6 m (25 ft)*
WEIGHT:	*2.4 tonnes (2¼ tons)*
DIET:	*Low-growing plants*

CLASSIFICATION

FAMILY:	*Nodosauridae*
INFRAORDER:	*Ankylosauria*
SUBORDER:	*Thyreophora*
ORDER:	*Ornithischia*

▶ MAP OF FINDS   ▶ COMPARE

△ *More than 50 dinosaurs feature in the Dinosaur Timeline that runs around the outer corridor. All the major dinosaurs are here, including familiar names like Tyrannosaurus Rex, and also Giganotosaurus, one of the most recent finds.*

PLAN

CRETACEOUS

WORLD OF DINOSAURS

dex

Dino Online

Store

MASKS

STATIONERY

POSTCARDS   ENVELOPES

WRITING PAPER   LABELS   INVITATIONS

△ *At the Museum Store you can download images or sounds to create stationery, masks, desktop patterns, or special effects.*

27

31 VIRTUAL MUSEUMS

Using 3-D graphics, multimedia architects can construct a "virtual" museum that exists only inside the computer. You can wander through the imaginary building, stopping to take in and interact with exhibits on the way.

△ EARTH QUEST
In this title, Eyewitness Virtual Reality Earth Quest *(Dorling Kindersley), you can visit the museum's virtual shop and "buy" stationery and souvenirs.*

◁ INTO THE EARTH
The program enables you to walk through a realistic 3-D building complete with museum-like displays. In the Earth Gallery, you can learn about gemstones.

32 "LIVE" ART GALLERIES

Museums house the world's finest collections of antiquities and art treasures – the one disadvantage is travelling to see them. With multimedia, you can look at the *Mona Lisa* in Paris and the dinosaur collection in the Smithsonian in Washington the same morning.

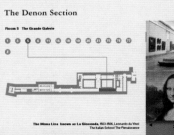

LE LOUVRE
BMG's Le Louvre *focuses on 100 of the museum's most significant paintings. From the main map, select which paintings to view.*

SCHOOL OF PAINTING   VIEW YOUR OWN CHOICE

33 LEISURE TITLES: WHAT'S AVAILABLE?

Leisure titles are among the fastest-expanding multimedia areas. The range of subjects now includes massage, beauty, and food; sports, from golf to football; more practical pursuits such as landscape and garden design; and hobbies – for example photography, guitar playing, and astrology. Specialization will increase as the market grows.

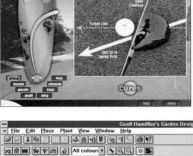

◁ PLAY BETTER GOLF (GSP)

▽ CINEMANIA (MICROSOFT®)

△ GEOFF HAMILTON'S GARDEN DESIGNER (GSP)

34 LIFESTYLE

Food and wine are enduringly popular subjects in publishing. With CD-Rom leisure titles you can learn to cook by watching top chefs, step by step, or learn how to assess wine from the expert on the screen in front of you. Microsoft® *Wine Guide* covers all aspects of wine, from where vines are grown to hints on tasting and serving wine. The title makes extensive use of video clips featuring wine expert, Oz Clarke.

INTERACTIVE WINE GUIDE
Oz Clarke acts as both guide and tutor in this wide-ranging title. Learn how to assess wine as well as gauging what to buy.

△ *Several hundred grape varieties are covered, with 12 well-known classics, including Sauvignon Blanc, described in detail.*

△ *Guides to reading the wine label are also a feature. Different labels are shown – click on the yellow circles to see more detailed information.*

◁ *The World Atlas of Wine provides interactive maps of the 12 major wine producing areas.*

35 SPORT

Sports enthusiasts who would like to improve their game can now enlist the aid of CD-Roms to help with skills and knowledge. GSP's *Play Better Golf* allows golf fans to watch and learn techniques through lessons and video clips, and by analysing champion golfers.

BRUSH UP YOUR TECHNIQUE

ON-SCREEN GARDEN PLANNING

36 PRACTICAL PURSUITS

Do-it-yourself skills and landscape design suit the CD-Rom format. *Geoff Hamilton's Garden Designer* (GSP) helps you to plan your garden on screen, and choose planting schemes. The title contains a plant encyclopedia, and options to see how your garden will look at night and in different seasons.

37 HOBBIES

Cinemania 97 (Microsoft®) offers a comprehensive guide to the world of film, making the most of CD-Rom's capacity to store video clips and dialogue. Cast lists and reviews are provided, along with photos and biographies of actors.

MICROSOFT® CINEMANIA 97

38 MULTI-SUBJECT ENCYCLOPEDIAS

The invention of the CD-Rom, with its capacity to store vast amounts of information, has been compared in significance to the invention of paper, the printing press, and photography. Although the book is certainly not dead, sound, speech, animation, and video can all be used to great effect on CD-Rom, bringing information to life in ways that would be impossible with the printed version. Encyclopedias adapt well to multimedia and are now key bestsellers in the market.

39 MICROSOFT® ENCARTA 97

Microsoft® *Encarta* is a popular multi-media encyclopedia using slide-down menus that appear when the pointer is moved. When the Pinpointer search tool is first opened, an alphabetical list of all *Encarta* articles appears. *Encarta 97* also includes an on-line link.

△ **WELCOME TO ENCARTA**
All information in Encarta *is classified into Areas of Interest and Categories.*

△ *The Pinpointer locates topics, but also contains features such as the ability to select pictures or sounds.*

△ *To locate the Hubble Space Telescope, just type the words at the top. There are 16 relevant articles.*

△ *Selecting Solar System from the Pinpointer accesses this screen, with images of the nine planets in the solar system. Click on each of the planets for more pictures and more detailed information.*

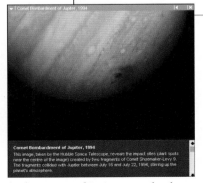

△ *This picture of Jupiter was taken by the Hubble Space Telescope in 1994. Click on Expand to see a bigger picture.*

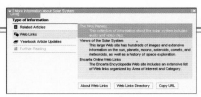

△ **Information** can be accessed in numerous different ways, and there are frequent links between topics. Encarta 97 can also be linked to the World Wide Web.

An **atlas** enables you to select a continent or country and then zoom in on a more detailed map. Views of the Seattle skyline can be seen by clicking on the Washington State map.

◁ **Coverage of historic** and world events is enhanced by video clips, photographs, and illustrations. Click on the Media icon for examples.

▽ **One video clip** shows the Hubble being repaired in space, and includes sound track of the astronauts.

△ **The first screen** has an up-to-date article with hypertext (Tip 20) and links to video, photographs, and animation.

△ **Animation can be** used to explain complex phenomena. Here, a moving solar system shows planets orbiting the sun.

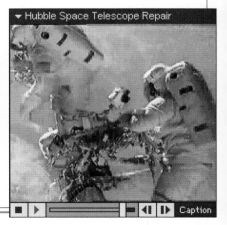

LEARNING THROUGH PLAY

40 WHAT IS EDUTAINMENT?

The best educational titles have gained from games titles – they are packed with colourful animation, sound, and video. Many of the most popular titles combine elements of *edu*cation and enter*tainment* so effectively that younger children are unaware that they are learning. Titles in this area fall into broad groups. Some help in a specific subject area, while others are more open-ended, and build on general thinking skills. Edutainment is now an important consideration for any family buying a multimedia computer.

SCIENCE ENCYCLOPEDIAS ▷

▽ TECHNOLOGY

△ CHILDREN'S DICTIONARIES   △ MULTILINGUAL VERSIONS

41 CREATIVE WRITING

Creativity titles usually provide libraries of images, sounds, animations, and text which a child can use in any combination. With more advanced titles, you can write storylines, and produce and direct animated cartoons or even create computer games. CD-Roms lend a new dimension to the traditional school activities of creative writing, art, and drama by encouraging a child to interact as well as create.

CREATIVE WRITER
With Microsoft's Creative Writer, *you can produce stories, newsletters, or family albums, using features from the Ideas Workshop.*

△ *The Ideas Workshop has two machines to help with writer's block. The Splot machine yields "wacky sentences" and the Picture Window "inspirational pictures".*

△ *Drop-down menus let you add colour and special effects, and also let you put in images to fit the words or replace them.*

△ *Images can be imported from the Picture Window to encourage children to start imagining the story immediately.*

42 MAKING CARTOONS

Children can create their own cartoons with titles such as Knowledge Adventure's *Spider-Man Cartoon Maker*, which uses figures and artwork from the TV series. A range of backgrounds, static objects, animations, and sounds enables players to "customize" a cartoon.

◁ *Assorted backgrounds can be chosen from this library of Spider-Man settings for each scene of the cartoon adventure.*

△ *These figures can be animated when they are dragged across the screen.*

SPIDER-MAN CARTOON MAKER

△ *You can assign musical themes to episodes in the new storyline.*

43 LANGUAGE LEARNING

Multimedia software can provide interactive and involving learning systems that parallel the way you learn a first language. EuroTalk's *Flashcards* teaches basic French through word/image association. You can record yourself, and test comprehension by playing learning games at your own pace.

PRACTICE & PLAYBACK

44 PRACTICE MAKES PERFECT

Anyone with a multimedia PC now has access to what was once possible only in a dedicated language lab. EuroTalk's *Aprende español con el hijo de Astérix* (Learn Spanish with Asterix's Son) presents a story in strip format using the familiar cartoon characters. Added features include screens with a record and playback facility for practising pronunciation.

◁ *This title uses modern, colloquial Spanish, and is aimed at learners who have mastered basic grammar.*

OPTIONS
The language of translation can be either British or American English, French, German, Portuguese, or Italian.

Learners can choose which part of the story to access, and whether they want speech, or text and speech. These buttons take you to the translation (traduccion) *and teacher's notes.*

▷ *On this screen, you can listen to the narration, then record and play back your own voice to practise your pronunciation.*

© LES EDITIONS ALBERT RENÉ, GOSCINNY-UDERZO

45 VOICE RECOGNITION

Most multimedia language-learning titles allow a learner to practise by recording and playing back speech, then comparing it with a model. The Learning Company's *French Vocabulary Builder* takes this a stage further, featuring voice recognition software that assesses a learner's pronunciation on a quality scale.

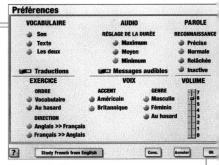

RECORD & PLAY
On this preferences screen, you specify how you want speech to be presented.

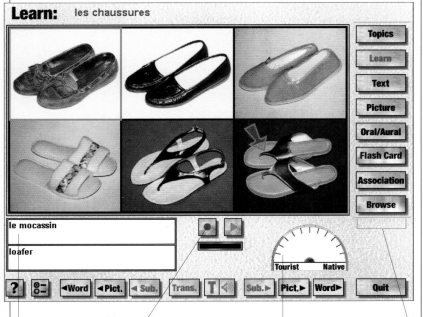

Record button

Each page *features a set of related images and words to learn and repeat.*

This dial passes judgment *on the authenticity of your accent, rating it on a scale from "tourist" to "native".*

Different activities, *based on the same sequence of illustrations, can be explored from these keys.*

46 LIVING BOOKS

Multimedia children's stories are inter-active versions of printed children's books, offering their users new worlds to explore and enjoy. They are simple to use, let children follow a story at their own pace, and can be extremely effective in teaching reading. *The Tortoise and the Hare*®, from Brøderbund's Living Books series, is based on the Aesop's fable of the same name. Children meet animated characters who pop up to embellish the main story with odd diversions.

OPENING THE DOOR
The young mouse realizes after three tries that she must say "please", as well as give the secret password.

After eating, the Hare felt very tired. So he decided to rest just for a little while. He immediately fell asleep. The Tortoise was surprised to find the Hare sleeping.

10

◁*As the hero* of the story, the tortoise defies all odds and wins the race against the hare through slow but steady progress.

▷*Simon the Storyteller*, a crow in red shoes, narrates the story. He appears in each scene, and adds his own comments on the tale.

47 GRAMMAR LESSONS

Brøderbund's *The Tortoise and the Hare®* uses the fable to teach and entertain. Two screens concentrate on the grammar of prepositions and verbs, using the tortoise and hare characters. Children can click on a word, hear it spoken, and see the meaning in animation.

LEARNING "UPHILL" ▷
To illustrate the meaning of the word "uphill", the tortoise is shown sweating as he struggles to climb.

△ **SKIPPING**
The hare performs a series of actions, illustrating the word "skip" energetically.

48 BASIC MATHS

Different multimedia titles teach maths in different ways. Some present activities that are modelled on a teacher at a blackboard, but using animated characters; others present maths as interactive games or puzzles. Other titles weave problem-solving into adventure games.

▽ **MATHS ACTIVITIES**
In Mathémagique® *(Maths Workshop) by Brøderbund, French-speaking children can explore mathematical ideas and develop problem-solving skills. Here, the Gorilla bowls for numbers.*

49 GAMES WITH NUMBERS

Dorling Kindersley's *I Love Maths* aims to reinforce all the key curriculum skills through involving children in time-travel rescue missions to ancient civilizations. Children learn about fractions by going to Atlantis to lay pipes and save the city from drought; learn about measurements as a judge at the Olympics in Greece; and work with geometric shapes to discover the secrets of an Aztec temple. The games can also be customized to cover specific school topics.

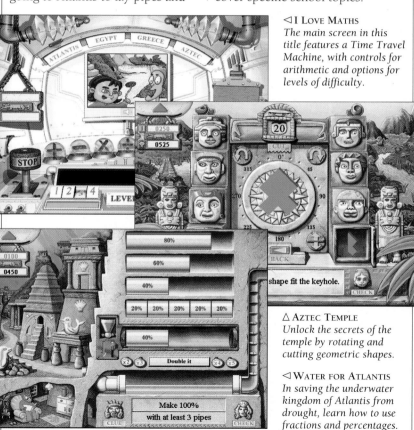

◁ **I LOVE MATHS**
The main screen in this title features a Time Travel Machine, with controls for arithmetic and options for levels of difficulty.

shape fit the keyhole.

△ **AZTEC TEMPLE**
Unlock the secrets of the temple by rotating and cutting geometric shapes.

◁ **WATER FOR ATLANTIS**
In saving the underwater kingdom of Atlantis from drought, learn how to use fractions and percentages.

50 ADVENTURES IN SCIENCE

Science titles aim to bring the subject to life by combining factual information with plenty of practical demonstrations. Some titles are based on "rooms" that you walk through and explore; others work like an interactive book, with topics and links to related subjects.

△ *Clicking on the "Map" icon takes you to a plan of the evo-dome. From here leap to other platforms.*

◁ LIFE SKILLS
In this title, The Evolution of Life with Richard Dawkins *(Notting Hill), the evolutionary biologist acts as your expert guide.*

HMS Beagle was a Royal navy survey ship. Charles Darwin was invited on board by her Captain, FitzRoy, who wanted a companion for the journey. He sailed with her for five years as the Beagle slowly worked her way around the world, mapping coastal waters, charting depths, and indicating great ocean currents.

Darwin was lucky to get the invitation. FitzRoy, a keen follower of the nineteenth-century fashion for physiognomy, suspected that his nose indicated laziness and hesitancy. This was soon disproved. Darwin was a keen collector and explorer. He often left the ship as it is sailed down the coast of South America, rejoining the vessel after long expeditions into the mountains and pampas.

△ *On Adaptation Island learn about species survival, and read about the life and work of Charles Darwin.*

△ *The title includes video footage as well as computer-simulated environments. At the base of the screen, click on the icons to return to the evo-dome, read more on the subject, scroll the screen or go back a step.*

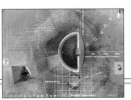

◁ *Learn about the eye by rotating the ball to see a three-dimensional model of its workings. See what happens when light enters.*

51 INTERACTIVE INVENTIONS

Dorling Kindersley's *The Way Things Work 2.0* focuses on an inventor's workshop, where different machines and other inventions are explored and can be animated. Other sections look at scientific principles. A Woolly Mammoth acts as a guide.

▽ **HISTORICAL TIMELINE**
A timeline, divided into phases such as the Industrial Revolution, places inventions in history.

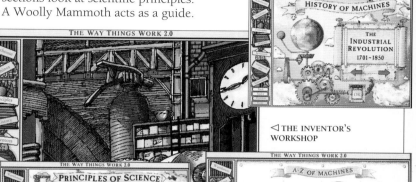

◁ **THE INVENTOR'S WORKSHOP**

An on-line facility links you to a regularly updated Web site on the Internet.

△ *In the A–Z of Machines, each machine can be located by choosing a letter of the alphabet. Click on a picture for more detail.*

The Woolly Mammoth *stars in short films that illustrate scientific principles such as heat.*

52 EARLY LEARNING

JumpStart Kindergarten, produced by Knowledge Adventure, groups three pre-school educational areas: simple learning, problem solving, and developing creativity. A cartoon rabbit called Mr Hopsalot acts as guide and teacher, offering instruction and advice but also plenty of praise and encouragement.

JUMPSTART KINDERGARTEN

ANIMATED CLOCK

53 TELLING THE TIME

The on-screen environment of *JumpStart Kindergarten* is very lively, with sounds and animation to hold (and keep) the child's attention. Clicking on the clock in the "classroom" takes you to exercises in telling the time. Daily activities are connected to times on the clock.

54 COLOURING

Creative activities in *Jump-Start Kindergarten* invite children to express themselves by choosing colours and words. Here, the child identifies the odd one out from a group of three images, then uses the palette to colour them in.

CHOOSING COLOURS

SIZING EXERCISE

55 PROBLEM-SOLVING

In this *JumpStart Kindergarten* activity, the child is asked to place a set of Russian dolls in order of relative size from large to small. A star appears in front of any doll placed in the correct position. Other exercises include grading a series of numbered blocks.

GAMES & ENTERTAINMENT

56 TYPES OF GAME

Computer games have developed almost as rapidly as the computer itself. From simple screen puzzles, multimedia machines are now powerful enough to produce realistic 3-D environments in which you can drive, fly, kill, and die. Today's games are both spectacular and involving, from violent action games (often called shoot 'em ups) to interactive films.

INTERNET GAMES
Many leading games companies use the World Wide Web to test their latest games, from chess to quizzes to adventure games, providing a rich source of on-line games for Internet users.

▽ DARK FORCES (LUCASARTS)

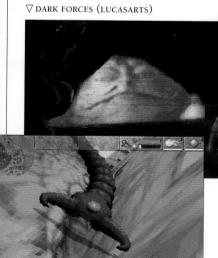

△ QUAKE (ID SOFTWARE)

△ MAGIC CARPET 2 (BULLFROG)

△ GAMES CONSOLE CARTRIDGES

57 PUZZLE GAMES

Computerized versions of tabletop war games were among the early computer games, later joined by fantasy role-playing games like *Dungeons and Dragons*. Multimedia adds a sense of being there by creating three-dimensional situations. In multimedia puzzles, real-world video sequences are combined with realistic graphics to create complete fantasy worlds. Brøderbund's *Myst®* places the player on a mysterious island.

MYST® (BRØDERBUND)
Myst *takes you to a surreal island and leaves you there. Few hints are given, and it is up to you to explore and solve clues. Pointing the hand-shaped cursor and clicking takes you to new locations.*

From the library, a path leads down to the shore. Across the water lies the clock tower. How do you get inside?

Once inside what looks like an air-raid shelter, a spiral passage takes you deeper into the ground.

Does the rocket work? Where could it take you?

Once you have lit the furnace in the log cabin, you can hear the fire roar. What is the energy being used for, though?

The library is where you start piecing together the puzzle, by interacting with objects and clues.

58 SHOOT 'EM UPS

Multimedia machines are now powerful enough to produce realistic environments in which you can drive, fly, kill, and die on screen. These games, known as shoot 'em ups, are often set in hostile underground labyrinths on distant planets or in vast space stations, where unknown hazards and enemies lurk around every corner. *Dark Forces*, shown below, is based on the *Star Wars* films.

DARK FORCES (LUCASARTS)

Stormtroopers need to be overcome to enter the room beyond.

The figures move so fast on screen that lavish detail is not necessary.

59 ACTIVITY GAMES

Titles based on flying or driving make greater demands on hardware than any other multimedia game. High-speed movement and instant reaction to the player's control are vital. Constant feedback is also a must, so that players can assess skill and success. Aerobatics such as rolls and spins also play a part in *Flight Unlimited*, by Looking Glass Technologies, which also has especially naturalistic terrain.

FLIGHT
UNLIMITED

60 MIXED-GENRE ADVENTURE GAMES

In *Star Trek: The Next Generation "A Final Unity"* (Spectrum Holobyte), based on the popular TV series, players looking for new challenges can opt for full control of the USS *Enterprise*, or simply explore the galaxy. The game uses elements from games and cartoons, but also from flight simulators and management training programmes.

MAIN SCREEN: USS ENTERPRISE BRIDGE
Clicking on certain areas of the main screen will allow you to access other important areas or functions of the ship.

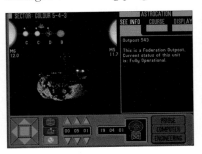

ASTROGATION
You need to know the three main control areas – Engineering, Astrogation, and Tactical – for full control. In Astrogation you can plot the course of the Enterprise, controlling direction and speed.

61 CARTOON ADVENTURES

Adventure games often take the form of interactive cartoons on CD-Rom, combining stereo sound with graphics and animations. *Full Throttle*, shown here, features the character Ben in a series of adventures. Explosive action sequences, a vibrant rock sound track, and unusual camera angles create considerable impact.

BEN: THE KEY CHARACTER

FULL THROTTLE (LUCASARTS) ▷

62 OTHER GAMES

The opportunities for technical innovation offered by CD-Rom mean that multimedia games have developed much more inventively than their nonelectronic predecessors. *Monty Python* (by 7th Level) is part-nostalgia, part-game.

MONTY PYTHON'S COMPLETE WASTE OF TIME
This surreal game takes the player into a world where insanity is a virtue. Chicken Man appears on screen at intervals to be used as target practice.

CHICKEN MAN

△ *Inside the* **Loonatorium** *(part of Mrs Zambesi's brain), you can play "Spot the Loony" – allegedly a very important aspect of the larger game.*

63 INTERACTIVE FILMS

An interactive film involves the player on several levels through use of extensive video sequences. You can watch the film unfold, and also direct the sequence of events. Some titles have a single plot line and it's up to the player to discover what that is. If the film has multiple plots, the storyline and the video that appear will depend on the choice the player has made. Sierra's *Phantasmagoria* is shown here.

PHANTASMAGORIA (SIERRA)
In this richly coloured title, Adrienne and Don have bought a vast house which has been empty for years. The player directs Adrienne as she explores. Here, she is using a poker to open a trapdoor.

PLAYER CHOICE
When making an interactive movie, each scene has to be filmed several times with different endings. Actors may betray or befriend people as directed by the player.

64 INTERACTIVE MUSIC

Most multimedia music CD-Roms include interactive elements of some kind. Some titles simulate the experience of working in a recording studio, allowing you to mix your own tracks. Others promote musicians and singers, by exploring a virtual world created from sound, interviews, and video clips related to their work. *Rock 'n Roll Your Own* from Compton's NewMedia is shown here.

You can use this button to record and play back sessions you are especially pleased with.

You can record new sounds or vocals using a microphone and your computer's sound card.

Add "scratch" effects by dragging the mouse over this area.

A keyboard facility lets you create your own tunes.

Each song section has its own video clip to go with it.

To insert a vocal sample, click on these buttons at any time during playback.

ROCK 'N ROLL YOUR OWN
This title presents eight songs and introduces some of the concepts that lie behind the digital editing of music.

The Songalizer enables you to choose the sequence in which your samples will be played.

65 DVD

A digital video disc (DVD) looks similar to a CD-ROM but has greater storage capacity and can play over 130 minutes of a feature film, with very good picture quality. In the future, DVD video discs will play on a computer equipped with a DVD-ROM drive.

66 HOME CONSOLES

Consoles are computers used primarily for playing games. Home consoles cost far less than a desktop computer, plug straight into a TV set, and offer instant entertainment without any computer know-how. The market really took off in the mid-1980s when Japanese manufacturers Nintendo and Sega brought out consoles.

△ SUPER NES CONSOLE (NINTENDO)

SEGA GENESIS ▷ (MEGADRIVE IN EUROPE)

IMPROVING BIT BY BIT
Early consoles had 4-bit processors, able to deal with only four bits of information at a time. The latest consoles have 32- or 64-bit main processors, with extra processors for sound and graphics.

67 CONSOLE CONTROL

Consoles are controlled using two-handed joypads, such as the Sega Saturn controller shown here. The buttons control direction of movement, game options, and actions. The number of buttons may have grown, but the basic design of a joypad has changed very little.

Gameplay buttons control actions within the game, such as making figures jump, fire, and punch.

The left-hand side controls direction of movement in a game. It may also control an on-screen pointer.

SEGA SATURN JOYPAD

---

68 ALTERNATIVE CONTROLS

Most multimedia computer games, played on a monitor, can be controlled with the usual keyboard and mouse; games consoles supply a range of alternative control methods. Most consoles are controlled using two-handed joypads, but the dedicated gamesplayer can also choose from racing-car steering wheels, aeroplane-style joysticks, and improved joypads or super joypads with extra buttons to make fighting moves.

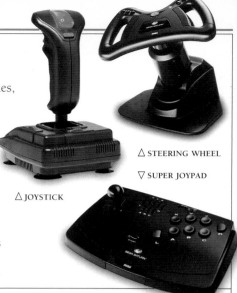

△ STEERING WHEEL

▽ SUPER JOYPAD

△ JOYSTICK

69 CONSOLE MASCOTS

The games console market was revived in the mid-1980s by Sega and Nintendo. The new 8-bit machines – the Sega Master System and the Nintendo Entertainment System (NES) – offered a level of speed and range of colours never seen before. Newer, 16-bit consoles were later launched, championed by their character mascots.

SONIC THE HEDGEHOG
Sega adopted a speedy hedgehog as the mascot for its 16-bit Genesis console.

SUPER MARIO
Nintendo chose an Italian plumber called Mario as the main character figure for its 16-bit Super NES games console.

70 SONY PLAYSTATION

The Sony PlayStation was released in Japan in 1994. Its powerful graphics processors are capable of realistic and very fast-moving 3-D images and the PlayStation's graphics were seen as incomparable when the console was first released. The joypad has a total of 14 fire and control buttons.

△ SONY PLAYSTATION

 The Sony PlayStation is powered by a 32-bit RISC chip capable of 30 million instructions per second.

 The PlayStation is capable of playing 24 channels of CD-quality sound.

 The PlayStation is dedicated to running games software, but can also play audio compact discs.

 The Sony PlayStation console has a double-speed CD-Rom drive for fast game loading.

 The graphics processors are designed for real-time 3-D animation using textures and shading.

Consoles can be linked with optional cables. An adapter allows eight players to use the console.

71 GAMES FOR PLAYSTATION

The Sony purchase of games-developer Psygnosis, producer of the highly popular game *Lemmings*, meant that the PlayStation has never been short of games. As well as racing and competing titles, there are action-packed adventures and games featuring martial arts.

DEMOLITION DERBY (PSYGNOSIS)

BATTLE ARENA TOSHINDEN (TAMSOFT)

72 SEGA SATURN

The Sega Saturn went on sale in Japan in 1994 and was an immediate success. It is mainly a games machine, but will also play audio CDs and Photo CDs with an adapter. With a video card it can play video CDs and interactive films. With a modem, it can access the Internet. An adapter enables up to 12 people to play at one time.

△ SEGA SATURN

◁ JOYPAD

 The Sega Saturn is powered by two 32-bit SH2 RISC processors, designed for Sega by Hitachi.

 The Yamaha sound card gives it 32 channels of CD-quality sound, MIDI music, and surround effects.

 Saturn titles are mostly games, but it can also play audio CDs, and Photo and video CDs (with adapter).

 The Sega Saturn has a double-speed CD-Rom drive with a dedicated processor and 512K cache.

 The Saturn has three graphics processors capable of producing fast 2-D and 3-D animation.

 The optional Net Link adapter gives the Saturn access to the Internet for multi-player gaming.

73 GAMES FOR SEGA SATURN

Sega Saturns are powerful enough to bring arcade games into the home. Over 200 titles are currently available for the console. The popular *Sega Rally* features fast-moving scenery and multi-player action. (A racing steering wheel is an optional extra.) *Virtua Fighter 2* is a hand-to-hand combat game with realistic fighting moves.

△ VIRTUA FIGHTER 2

SEGA RALLY ▽▷

VIRTUAL REALITY

74 WHAT IS VIRTUAL REALITY?

Virtual reality is a form of technology which combines computer graphics, video, stereo sound, and stereo display. With a headset incorporating two small video screens, the player can enter and explore a computer-generated, interactive, 3-D environment. Once used only for flight simulators, virtual reality is now used to plan new buildings, test cars, train the military, and in fantasy games.

◁ VIRTUAL CAR
Cars can be test-driven using a simulator and a virtual reality headset. Drivers can also be tested.

▽ IN A DIFFERENT WORLD
Players feel as though they are completely surrounded by a virtual landscape.

◁ MAGIC CARPET 2
This title from Bullfrog can be played on screen or by using a virtual reality headset.

55

75 VIRTUAL REALITY IN YOUR OWN HOME

Once able to run only on expensive workstations, virtual reality was confined to research laboratories. However, with the increase in power of personal computers, it is now possible to experience virtual reality technology with a desktop computer or games console. Low-cost headsets are widely available, and an increasing number of software applications have been written to take advantage of them. In the future, devices that can simulate movement, and even smell and touch could become available.

76 ARCADE MACHINES

Using virtual reality can be a bizarre experience. Instead of looking at a computer-generated world, you feel you are inside a real world. You can pick up an object, or open a door. If you tilt your head back, you see what is above you. Virtual reality arcade machines typically consist of a pod surrounded by a protective barrier. With a headset and a pointer, the player begins a game. The more powerful the computer, the more realistic the game.

▽ GHOST TRAIN, FROM VIRTUALITY
In this game, players are taken on a white-knuckle roller-coaster ride through a world inhabited by monsters and skeletons.

▽ SAFETY MEASURES
Playing a virtual game can be very disorienting. The Series 2000 game pods from Virtuality surround the player with a barrier.

77 SIMULATING ENVIRONMENTS

With its effective simulation of three-dimensional space, virtual reality is ideal for displaying information spatially, and has many practical applications. Combat pilots can do initial training safely on the ground in a flight-simulation system rather than in expensive jet fighters. Soldiers can use it to practise firing new weapons; pilots to prepare for battle situations; and officers to improve strategy.

BATTLE SIMULATION
Simulating realistic battle situations, virtual reality is widely used by the armed forces to train pilots and soldiers.

78 COMPUTER-AIDED DESIGN

A major use of virtual reality technology is computer-aided design (CAD). One example of CAD is the architectural walk-through, where an architect's data for a building is used to create a 3-D virtual construction. By wearing a headset, clients can "tour" a building before it is built, gaining a much more realistic idea of its shape, size, and character than would be possible from viewing drawings or models. Similar virtual reality techniques are used by engineers to plan the construction and maintenance of nuclear power plants.

▽ **VIRTUAL PLANT**
Engineers can visualize inside complex structures, such as a nuclear reactor.

△ **IDEAL HOME**
Coordinates are manipulated to create a 3-D house you can "visit".

MULTIMEDIA ON THE WEB

79 WHAT IS THE WORLD WIDE WEB?

For many people, the World Wide Web is the most exciting aspect of the Internet. The Web is a universe of linked "pages", and you navigate it as you would a multimedia CD-Rom. A typical Web page contains words and pictures, like a magazine, but with the big difference that the page is interactive, and may contain sound, video clips, and links to other pages. To access the World Wide Web, all you need is a standard Internet connection and some "browser" software (*Tip 81*). There are millions of pages to explore.

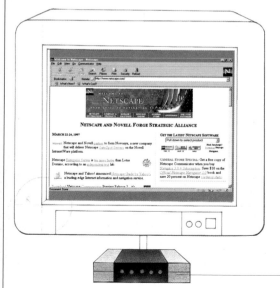

ISDN
The Integrated Services Digital Network (ISDN) provides one of the fastest links to the Internet for home users. It transmits using existing phone lines.

ON-LINE MULTIMEDIA
Anything that can be stored on a CD-Rom can also be sent over a phone line or television cable.

A modem (MOdulator-DEModulator) lets you access the Internet and on-line services from a computer, converting binary data to an analogue signal and vice versa.

80 ON-LINE SERVICE PROVIDERS

On-line Service Providers (OSPs) differ from Internet Service Providers (ISPs) in that OSPs offer a privately maintained network, as well as access to the Internet. OSP customer-only features include access to news services, up-to-date stock market prices, encyclopedias, dictionaries, and airline and railway timetables. You can also engage in on-line chatting, and communicate with others by electronic mail. OSP networks share many Internet features, but are often more logical and user-friendly environments, especially for newcomers.

MINITEL
One of the earliest on-line services was Minitel, set up by France Telecom in 1982. Everyone in France was given a terminal, free, in a move to upgrade the entire nation's technology.

◁ OSP: COMPUSERVE

▽ OSP: MSN™, THE MICROSOFT® NETWORK

◁ OSP: AMERICA ONLINE

81 WEB BROWSERS

Initially, a Web browser was simply a tool for viewing pages on the Web. Today's Web browsers are much more than Web navigation tools: they have developed into launchpads from which you can send e-mail and visit newsgroups. Two leading Web browsers are *Microsoft® Internet Explorer* and *Netscape Navigator*, which show you how to navigate the Web. They also come with plug-ins (*Tip 86*).

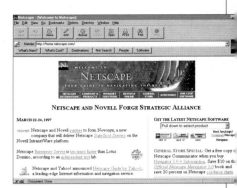

NETSCAPE NAVIGATOR (NETSCAPE CORPORATION)

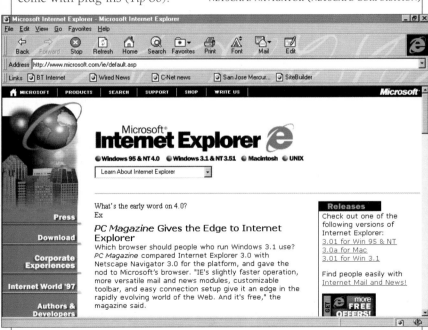

△ MICROSOFT® INTERNET EXPLORER

82 SEARCH TOOLS

Exploring the Web is made more manageable by the existence of search tools. The two main types are Web directories (lists of topics like a huge index) and search engines, which follow your typed instructions. Shown here are some search tools with Internet addresses.

nln.com

guide.infoseek.com

www.100hot.com

www.excite.com

altavista.digital.com

www.lycos.com

83 MAGAZINES ON THE WEB

Multimedia magazines offer readers a completely new way to interact with a magazine's contents. Magazines on CD-Rom have given way to magazines on the Web, which offer interactive editions of existing publications, with added video and sound. Hypertext links enable you to search for particular topics, in current and back issues.

84 JAVA

Java is a programming language that enables Web pages to contain miniature programs – called applets – that appear as animation, sound, scrolling text, or interactive features like functional spread-sheets. Java has revolutionized the Web for both users and developers. Your Web browser needs to be Java-enhanced if you want to view Java applets.

ALL ABOUT JAVA

85 ACTIVEX

ActiveX controls are similar to Java applets (*Tip 84*), except that when you encounter one on a Web page, you are asked whether you wish to download it. If you accept, it will automatically be integrated into your operating system, becoming active if needed.

ABOUT ACTIVEX

86 PRE-INSTALLED PLUG-INS

A pre-installed plug-in is simply a program that adds capabilities to your Web browser (*Tip 81*). It may improve the ability to handle video, animation, games, or interactive documents. The latest versions of *Netscape Navigator* and *Microsoft Internet Explorer* come with plug-ins. If a Web browser cannot locate the appropriate plug-in, you will need to download the one you require separately.

87 VRML PROGRAMS

A Virtual Reality Modelling Language (VRML) program allows you to explore virtual worlds (*Tip 90*) and play with three-dimensional images on the Internet. *Viscape*, by Superscape, shown here, is a proprietary 3-D system. Download it from http://www.superscape.com.

NAVIGATING IN 3-D
In this example, you have a 360-degree range of movement. Use the controls to explore.

Move up or down, or left or right

Look up or down

With this button, go left, right, back, or forward

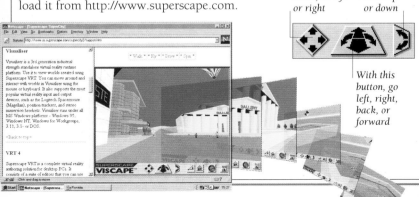

88 NEW PLUG-INS

There are hundreds of plug-ins available that will increase the functionality of your Web browser, with new ones appearing regularly. Most plug-ins are self-extracting files that are very easy to install. You just need to download the plug-in software and install it on your hard disk. This selection is compatible with Windows 95.

▽ SHOCKWAVE
This Macromedia plug-in enables you to view animation and film, and hear high-quality sound.

△ SHOCKWAVE IN ACTION
Shockwave enables you to appreciate this MB Interactive Web site with its interactive rhythm machine.

AUDIO & VIDEO

Crescendo
Crescendo allows you to play stereo MIDI music.
http://www.liveupdate.com/midi.html

Intervu MPEG Player
This enables you to play MPEG audio-video files.
http://www.intervu.com/player/player.html

Apple QuickTime
To view films on Web sites.
http://www.quickTime.apple.com/sw/

3-D & ANIMATION

CosmoPlayer
A VRML 2.0(Tip 87) viewer.
http://vrml.sgi.com/cosmoplayer

VRScout
For interacting with 3-D locations and objects.
http://www.chaco.com/vrscout/

Shockwave Splash
Use to view animated graphics and drawings.
http://www.macromedia.com/software/flash

OTHER PLUG-INS

Pointcast Network
This offers constantly updated news, weather, sports, and financial news.
http://www.pointcast.com

FormulaOne/Net
To view Microsoft Excel-compatible spreadsheets.
http://www.visualcomp.com/f1net/download.htm

IPIX
Navigate within a totally immersive 360° environment. http://www.ipix.com/

89 PLAYING ON-LINE GAMES

The Net provides a treasure house of gaming resources – new software, add-ons for commercial games, hints, tips, and cheats. The most exciting aspect is the chance to pit your skill against other players in one-to-one or multiplayer games. *Microsoft Internet Gaming Zone*, below, is one site where you can play immediate-response games.

△ *Once inside* Checkers, *simply drag and drop the counters to make moves. Chat by typing in the box.*

△ *Double-click on an empty seat to begin a game. Double-click on a person to view a game in progress.*

△ *Buildings in the Village area have rooms devoted to games such as chess, bridge, or draughts (checkers).*

90 EXPLORING VIRTUAL WORLDS

In 1995, the arrival of "cyber-worlds" or "virtual multiuser environments" made on-line chat even more involving. Users are depicted on-screen by graphic "avatars"; you choose your own look. Fujitsu Cultural Technologies' *WorldsAway* is set in the virtual city of Phantasus. The 3-D world of *Worlds Chat* is a space station.

WORLDSAWAY (FUJITSU)

WORLDS CHAT (WORLDS INC.)

MULTIMEDIA SERVICES

FIBRE-OPTIC CABLES
Fibre-optic cable is made of strands of extremely pure glass, capable of carrying phenomenal amounts of digital data.

```
0010101
0101011101000
1001010010100001
00100100111011010
1001010010100001
0101011101000
0010101
```

DIGITAL DATA

91 THE NOT-SO-SUPERHIGHWAY?

A high-capacity communications network (also called a broadband network) could carry vast amounts of digital binary data in and out of every home. The Internet is often seen as a prototype information superhighway, but the future depends on whether broadband services really give value for money.

92 POINT-OF-SALE KIOSKS

Kiosks can be used to sell anything from furniture to washing machines, and are very useful in areas that are far from shopping centres. Customers choose from text menus or screen pictures. Many point-of-sale kiosks use a touch screen with on-screen prompts to help buyers who are unfamiliar with computers.

△ **Type the title** of the book or video desired by touching the keyboard.

△ **Clear categories** make it easy for users to search through video titles.

△ **On this screen,** the image of a bookshelf starts you off on a book search.

93 INTERACTIVE TV

Unlike broadcast television, an interactive service allows the customer to choose which service to use at any given time, whether it's shopping, watching a film, or playing games. Providing interactive services is both an impressive feat of engineering – and a costly one. Trials are under way around the world to find out which service people are prepared to pay for.

△ SERVICES ON TRIAL
The Time-Warner Cable trial uses a carousel as a revolving display of services.

SHOPPERVISION BY TIME-WARNER CABLE

94 VIRTUAL SUPERMARKET

The home shopping service offered by interactive TV is more flexible than home shopping TV channels. You can enter virtual shops and examine goods, read details on the packaging, and simply press a button to order. Your credit card is debited, and the goods delivered.

95 VIDEO-ON-DEMAND

Video-on-demand provides the film you want to watch, instantaneously. Using a remote control from a service provider, you choose a subject category, then select a film from an electronic video shop. Once selected, you can then stop the film, pause it, rewind it, or fast forward, just as though you had the actual tape in your video recorder.

ENDLESS CHOICE
Choose from an extensive list of films with Time-Warner Cable's interactive service.

NEAR VIDEO-ON-DEMAND
Some satellite television services offer "near video-on-demand". A development of pay-per-view systems seen on cable TV, this service offers a selection of films that start every 15 or 30 minutes.

96 INTERNET TELEPHONES

Internet technology allows you to phone anyone with an Internet link, anywhere in the world, using your multimedia PC. Internet telephony programs work by first digitizing your speech, spoken into the PC's microphone, then sending voice data across the Internet. Your PC rings to indicate connection. If the person you call is not on-line, you can leave a message on voice mail.

USING DIGIPHONE AT HOME
With a product like DigiPhone, you can talk long-distance for the price of a local call.

97 OTHER ON-DEMAND SERVICES

On-demand services could do away with the need for printed television schedules. Interactive television users can already call up news-on-demand, and sport-on-demand is also possible. Most trials also offer the chance to try out different games, which are sent to the set-top box and can be played alone, or by linking to the network.

MAIN MENU
British Telecom's pilot scheme uses icons on the main screen to present choices.

VIDEO GAMES
A range of 64-bit action games with 3-D images is on offer from Time-Warner Cable.

TOUCHPOINT

98 PUBLIC INFORMATION

It is now common to see public kiosks that use touch screens, graphical interfaces, and video telephones to provide information about goods and services. Most systems run on a computer inside a kiosk, and use the latest multimedia to improve and expand the service. More advanced kiosks offer features such as printers and credit card readers.

TOUCHPOINT FROM BT
Just touch the screen to book tickets, buy goods, or access eight channels of services.

99 IN-FLIGHT MULTIMEDIA

Many international airlines use in-flight multimedia to make long journeys more enjoyable for passengers. You can now view films on demand, play computer games, or "shop" from a selection of options, all from the comfort of your own seat. Screens are in front of you, and a controller is attached to the armrest. An onboard computer controls the system, linked to the ground by satellite. Passengers can also make international calls, and chart their flight on screen.

◁ MULTIMEDIA CENTRE
On this Virgin flight, passengers can access a host of services.

△ IN CONTROL
One side of the remote is like a phone pad, the other is a games controller.

100 VIDEOCONFERENCING

Home users may have been slow to take up videophones, yet existing technology now makes possible international video meetings, without the expense or delay of travel. Videoconferencing also brings benefits to remote areas, where schools and medical centres can benefit from computer links.

△ FACE-TO-FACE
Broadband computer networks and digital cameras provide high-quality links for successful long-distance meetings.

◁ NOW YOU SEE ME
Videophones, multimedia e-mail, and videoconferencing are all now familiar in the workplace.

MULTIMEDIA NEWS
Personalized newspapers with video and sound could be assembled electronically by "intelligent searchers".

101 SMART APPLIANCES

On-line and virtual reality equipment may make it easier to pursue much of our business without stirring from home. There are likely to be further links between different technologies, particularly television, computer, and telephone. Powerful home computers will be capable of controlling TVs and VCRs, heating and humidity, and will be linked by cable to the superhighway.

INDEX

ACKNOWLEDGMENTS

Dorling Kindersley would like to thank Hilary Bird for compiling the index, Polly Boyd for proof-reading, Richard Hammond for editorial help, Robert Campbell for DTP assistance, and Aura Multimedia, Anna Milner, David Arscott, Tim Worsley, Huw Clough, Joe Elliot, and Valerie Buckingham for their invaluable help and advice.

Photography & Illustrations

KEY: t *top*; b *bottom*; c *centre*; a *above*; l *left*; r *right*.

The publisher would like to thank the following for their kind permission to reproduce their photographs: **Bridgeman Art Library, London:** *Self Portrait as a Young Man* 1634 by Rembrandt 11tl; **BT Corporate Picture Library;** a **BT** photograph: 8c, 67bl, 68tr, 69tr & cla; **DigiPhone Europe Limited:** 67tr; **Encyclopaedia Britannica International Ltd:** 12tl; **Virgin Atlantic Airways Ltd:** 68bl.

The publisher would like to thank the following copyright holders for their kind permission to reproduce their screengrabs/products, all of which are trademarks: "AOL" and the AOL triangle logo are registered trademarks of **America Online, Inc.** All rights reserved: 59bl; **Atari Corporation:** 67br; **BMG Interactive:** 28br; **Brøderbund:** 6cl, 8tr, 39c, 40tr & b, 46; **Bullfrog:** 45bl, 55bl; **Bungie Software:** 8br; Permission granted by **CompuServe Incorporated.** Thank you to CompuServe (Information Services) UK for their help: 13br, 59cla, 64bl; Screen shots taken from 3D Atlas courtesy of **Creative Wonders.** © 1997 Creative Wonders. All rights reserved: 24c & b, 25; **DIGITAL,** AltaVista and the AltaVista logo are trademarks or service marks of **Digital Equipment Corporation.** Used with permission: 61ca; **Division Limited:** 55cl & br, 57tr, bl, & br; **EuroTalk Limited:** 8cr, 36br, 37; © 1996 by **Excite:** 61cla; **Global Software Publishing:** 29tl & b, 31tr & cl; **id:** 12bl, 45cr; Reprinted by permission. Infoseek, Ultrasmart, iSeek, Quickseek, Imageseek, Ultrashop, "proof of intelligent life on the net" and Infoseek logos are trademarks of Infoseek Corporation which may be registered in certain jurisdictions. Other trademarks shown are trademarks of their respective owners. Copyright © 1995–1997 **Infoseek Corporation.** All rights reserved.: 61tl; **IVI Publishing:** 5cl; JumpStart Kindergarten, courtesy of Knowledge Adventure Inc. TM and © 1994 **Knowledge Adventure Inc.** All rights reserved: 42, 44; Spider-Man Cartoon Maker, courtesy of Knowledge Adventure, Inc. © 1995 **Knowledge Adventure Inc.** All rights reserved. TM and © **Marvel Characters, Inc.** All rights reserved: 8bl, 36t; **The Library Corporation:** 61tl; **The Learning Company:** 16c, 38c, 50c; Courtesy of **LucasArts Entertainment Company:** *Dark Forces*™ and © 1994 Lucasfilm Ltd. All rights reserved. Used Under Authorization: 12br, 45cl, 47t; *Full Throttle®* & © 1994 LucasArts Entertainment Company. All rights reserved. Used Under Authorization 48br; © 1996 **Macromedia Inc.** All rights reserved. Shockwaves is a trademark of Macromedia Inc: 63cl; © **M/B Interactive Inc.** All Music by Akio Akashi: 63cra; **MicroProse:** 48cla; Screen shots reprinted by permission from **Microsoft Corporation:** 5cl, 14tr, 21bl & cr 29cr, 30cl, 31bl, 32–33, 35, 59br, 60b, 62tr, 64t; **Muze Inc:** 65b, Copyright 1996 **Netscape Communications Corp.** Used with permission. All Rights Reserved. This page may not be reprinted or copied without the express written permission of Netscape: 58cb, 60tr; **Nintendo/THE Games:** 52br; **Notting Hill Electronic Publishing:** 42c; Screenshots of Destruction Derby © 1996 **Psygnosis Limited.** All rights reserved: 53bl; Sega and SEGA SATURN are trademarks of **SEGA ENTERPRISES, Ltd:** 52bl, 54cl, br, & bc; **7th Level:** 49tr & cla; **Sierra Online:** 49clb & br; **Smithsonian Institution:** 10cr & bl; **Sony Computer Entertainment UK/Tokara Co. plc:** 53br; © 1996, **Superscape VR plc:** 62bl; Used by permission of **Sun Microsystems Inc.** Copyright 1997 Sun Microsystems, Inc. 2550 Garcia Ave. Mtn. View, CA 94043-1100 USA, All rights reserved: 61br; **Time Warner Cable FSN:** 7cr, 66tr, cl, & br; **Virgin Interactive:** 47br; **Virtuality:** 7tl, 56bl & br; **Voyager:** 19c, 24tr; **Web21** of Palto Alto, California, makers of the 100hot websites, a distinguished directory of the net, can be reached at www.100hot.com: 61tr; Worlds Chat Screen Grabs © 1996, **Worlds Inc:** 64br; **Xebec (Multimedia Solutions):** 9bl & br; Text and artwork copyright © 1996 by **YAHOO! Inc.** All rights reserved. YAHOO! and the YAHOO! logo are trademarks of YAHOO! Inc: 61ca.

Cover: Fractal Design Corporation: inside front; **Virtuality:** back cra; **Xebec (Multimedia Solutions):** back bl.